Around the Pond in 80 Days

A musical for children

Shrubshall and Free

Samuel French — London
www.samuelfrench-london.co.uk

AROUND THE POND IN 80 DAYS

First performed by Year 6 of Bonner Primary School, Bethnal Green and by Year 6 of Ibstock Place School, Roehampton, in 2004. Subsequently it was showcased with an adult cast and a children's chorus from Deansfield Primary School at Greenwich Theatre in 2005.

STAGING NOTES

The Set

Around The Pond In 80 Days is written to be performed on a sparsely furnished stage. The overall look can suggest a pond-side environment, but each scene is set in dialogue and needs only the odd table or chair as embellishment.

Staging Suggestions

The script contains notes on all the staging elements that are necessary for a production. The suggestions below are optional additions to those in the script.

The Dragonfly Chorus (SCENE 2)
The dragonfly chorus could carry large model dragonflies suspended from poles by fishing line.

The Firefly Chorus (SCENE 4)
The firefly chorus could carry glow-sticks or torches which they could twirl around.

The Boats (SCENES 5 and 13) and Balloon Basket (SCENE 7)
In SCENE 5, Phil and the gang could enter on a trolley dressed as a wrecked boat and pulled on by the sticklebacks. The trolley could then be redressed as the balloon basket for SCENE 7 and again as a boat in SCENE 13.

The Mosquitoes (SCENE 6)
The mosquitoes might wear dark glasses with a long proboscis attached.

Rainstorm (SCENE 7)
Rainsticks and thunderboards could represent the rainstorm instead of recorded effects.

The Falling Balloon (SCENE 8)
A model balloon — possibly with model frogs and a model snake in it — could fall on a wire in view of the Fisherman.

AROUND THE POND IN 80 DAYS

This musical is written to be performed by a cast of children, Years 6-9/ages 10-14. It can also be performed by a cast of eight adults with doubling or with a children's chorus.

NB The accents mentioned below are merely suggestions. Regional or national variations may be used freely to enhance the sense of a journey.

Amphibia
Phileas Frog, (aka **Phil**) our intrepid hero
Pass, Phil's faithful, fat, friend (possibly with a French accent)
Phoebe, a frog princess
Fix, (female) a sneaky snake in the grass
Fink, boss of the lily-pad factory
Frogs 1, 2, 3, 4, 5
Frog Chorus

The Reed Bed
Dragonfly Chorus

A Milk Bar in Wartville
Toadettes 1, 2, 3 and 4, a girl gang, possibly with US accents
Waiter
Nat Natterjack, the king of the toads

Rocky Shore
Lead Crayfish ⎫
Various Crayfish ⎬ Mexican accents
Firefly Chorus ⎭

Stickleback Shallows
Big Stickle, a wise, old stickleback
Little Stickle, a silly, young stickleback
Stickle 1, 2
Stickleback Chorus

The Swamp
Mosquito Chorus

Newtopia
Franklin Newt
Babbage Newt } eminent scientific newts
Hodgkin Newt
Capability Newt
Newt Chorus

The Balloon Flight
Fisherman

The Waterfall
Wavemakers
Ol' Pikey

Ratsburg
Prosecutor
Lawyer Rat
Judge Rat
Water Rat Chorus

THE SONGS

1. **Overture / Riveting Chorus**   Phil, Pass and Frog Chorus

2. **Around the Pond**   Phil, Pass, Fink and Frog Chorus

3. **80 Days (2-6)**   Phil, Pass and Dragonfly Chorus

4. **Snake in the Grass**   Fix, Phil and Pass

5. **King of the Toads**   Toadettes, Nat Natterjack and Pass

6. **My One True Frog**   Phoebe

7. **Crayfish**   Lead and Various Crayfish

8. **80 Days (15)**   Firefly Chorus

9. **Stickleback Chorus**   Stickleback Chorus

10. **Ol' Pikey**   Big and Little Stickle, Stickle 1, 2 and Stickleback Chorus

11. **80 Days (34-40)**   Mosquito Chorus

12. **Rise Up Toward the Sun**   Franklin, Babbage, Hodgkin and Capability Newt, Phil, Pass, Phoebe, Fix and Newt Chorus

13. **The Waterfall**   Wavemakers

14. **80 Days (60-70)**   Prosecutor and Water Rat Chorus

15. **The Pursuit of Flies**   Phil, Phoebe, Fix, Judge Rat, Prosecutor and Water Rat Chorus

16. **80 Days (71-79)**   Phil, Phoebe, Pass, Fix and Various Creatures

17. **Around the Pond: Reprise**   Fink, Frog and Stickleback Chorus, Phil, Phoebe, Pass and Fix

Amphibia

A pond-side environment

The play begins in darkness. A chorus of frogs, plus Phil and Pass, are on stage with their lunchboxes nearby. Pass's lunchbox is extra large. A knapsack is set to one side of the stage

Song 1: Overture / Riveting Chorus

From the darkness, we hear the familiar sound of frogs "riveting". Groups of frogs sing in canon

Phil	
Pass	Rivet, rivet, rivet …
1st Frogs	
2nd Frogs	Rivet …
Phil	
Pass	Rivet …
1st Frogs	
2nd Frogs	Rivet …

The Lights gradually come up. We see that the frogs are not just sitting about croaking but are making mechanical movements as if working in a factory, riveting together a large lily pad. Each time a frog says "rivet", another frog provides a (mimed) rivet to put in place

Phil	
Pass	Rivet …
1st Frogs	
3rd Frogs	Rivet …
2nd Frogs	Rivet …
Phil	
Pass	Rivet …
1st Frogs	
3rd Frogs	Rivet …
2nd Frogs	Rivet…

*Fink enters, carrying a fob watch, and surveys the scene. He doesn't seem
too happy with the workers — especially Phil. Fink checks his watch and
signals off stage*

Phil	
Pass	Rivet …
1st Frogs	
3rd Frogs	Rivet …
2nd Frogs	Rivet …
4th Frogs	Rivet …
Phil	
Pass	Rivet …
1st Frogs	
3rd Frogs	Rivet …
2nd Frogs	Rivet …
4th Frogs	Rivet …

A whistle sounds, bringing the song to an end

Fink Riveting tools away, frogs. Lunchtime.

The frogs down tools and open up their lunchboxes

Phil Come on, Pass, let's sit under the great oak.

Phil and Pass sit down to eat

Pass I am frog tired. We must have riveted twenty lily pads today already.
Phil But it's rewarding — helping young froglets get a flipper on the property
ladder.
Pass Yes, but it sure makes me hungry.
Phil Everything makes you hungry, Pass. I think even eating makes you
hungry.
Pass (*taking a large baguette out of his box*) You're probably right, Phil. But
who can resist succulent spiders in a delicious buguette with some dry
roasted gnats? (*He eats the baguette during the following*)
Phil And for the moment we can just lie back and enjoy the sunshine. We've
got a whole hour before we have to…
Fink Just half an hour for lunch today, frogs. You're falling behind. (*To
Phil*) And only fifteen minutes' break for you, Phileas Frog – don't think
I haven't seen you day-dreaming all morning.
Phil Sure thing, Mr Fink.
Fink (*to Pass*) And young Pass. I see that once again you've brought lunch
for everyone. (*Pretending surprise*) Oh, it's all for you, is it? Well, no

wonder you're getting so fat, Pass. You know, pretty soon you'll be so big you'll be able to *pass* for a toad. (*Laughing*) *Pass* for a toad, my word.

Pass gets angry; Phil calms him. Fink goes to bother somebody else

Pass One day I'll show that bully, Fink. I'll walk out of here and tell him what he can do with his crummy job. One day — when I earn enough money.
Phil Sure, Pass. One day.
Pass But I have to do this, Phil. What about you? You've already riveted yourself the best pad in Amphibia. Why do you put up with Fink always picking on you?
Phil I enjoy the work. And I enjoy the company, Pass. Anyway, what else would I do? Just sit alone on my luxury pad and twiddle my thumbs. (*He tries to twiddle his thumbs, then realizes frogs don't have thumbs*)
Pass You could go travelling like you've always wanted. You could leave Amphibia. Have an adventure.
Phil (*after a moment's thought*) Hm, I did always have an idea about someday going all the way around the pond.

The Frogs sitting nearby start to laugh

Pass (*to the laughing Frogs*) And what's so funny about that?
Frog 1 Going around the pond? It's impossible to go around the pond.
Frog 2 There are great forests and vast swamps…
Frog 3 Huge mountains and wide canyons…
Frog 4 And terrible beasts that just love the taste of frog meat.
Frog 5 Some say the pond's so big it flows off the edge of the world.

The Frogs nod in awe. Fink listens in during the following

Phil That's just silly superstition. If the pond flowed off the edge of the world all the water would have disappeared by now. No, judging by the curve of the bank, I've calculated that an average frog, travelling at no more than hopping pace, would probably be able to go around the pond in less than twelve weeks.

The Frogs laugh at him

Really!

Even Pass looks a little unconvinced

Fink Prove it.

Phil But it's hard to understand, it's all to do with maths and angles and stuff. I've got some calculations back at my pad …

Fink Ooh, maths and angles — calculations — *we* wouldn't understand. That's what I've always disliked about you, Phileas. You think you're better than all of us, there on your luxury pad with your books and your plans and your foolish dreams. Well, I just dare you to go around the pond. I just dare you.

Phil is put on the spot. Fink and the Frogs laugh

Song 2: Around the Pond

Pass (*speaking*) No, Phil. I know what you're thinking, but it's madness.

Frogs (*singing*)
Phileas, Phileas,
Phileas Frog,
Phileas Frog,
Phileas Frog is the sillies' frog,
The sillies' frog is Phileas,
Phileas Frog.

Phil (*speaking*) Right, Fink. I'll show you!
(*Singing*) I'm going around the pond…

Pass	Around the pond? Around the pond…?
Phil	As if without a care …
Pass	Have a care, please take care.
Phil	With a skip and a jump, but mainly a hop,
	I'm on my way and no-one can stop
	This grand adventure started by a dare…
Pass	But Phileas, why are you going around the pond?
Phil	Because it's there.
Frogs	He's going around the pond…
Phil |	
Pass |	Around the pond, around the pond…
Frogs	He must be hopping mad…
Phil |	
Pass |	Maybe mad, just a tad…
Frogs	He'll fall down a hole,
	Get eaten by snakes;
	We're telling you, Phil,
	To put on the brakes,
	We're sure the end you'll come to will be bad…
Fink	So Phileas, what are you risking on the bet?
	If you don't return what do I get?
Phil	Well, Fink, I'll bet my luxury pad.

The Frogs all gasp in surprise

During the following, Pass tries to talk Phil out of the bet

Frogs	Phileas Frog has lost his mind,
	The silliest frog you'll ever find;
	He's bet his home on a one-way trip,
	He's sure to stumble, fall or slip,
	And when he does,
	When he does,
	When he does,
	His pad is in Fink's grip.
Fink	So when can I take possession of my prize, Phileas?
	I don't want to stand around just catching flies, Phileas?
Phil	I'll be back before you know it, Fink, you'll see ——
	Before the last leaf's fallen from the great oak tree.

The Frogs gasp — it can't possibly be done

Fink (*speaking; laughing*) You foolish, foolish frog. If you make it round in that time, why I'll give everyone the week off and do the riveting myself.
Phil It's a deal.

Phil shakes hands with Fink

Pass Phil, are you mad? That's only eighty days away.
Phil So I've no time to lose. (*He heads off*)
Pass But don't you think you'll at least need an overnight bag?
Phil (*stopping*) Oh, yes, I suppose so.
Pass (*shrugging*) Looks like you might need some help. I'd better come along too.
Phil Really, Pass? That's fantastic.

Phil **Pass**	(*singing*) We're going around the pond…
Frogs **Fink**	Around the pond, around the pond.
Phil **Pass**	As if without a care …
Frogs **Fink**	Not a care, not a care.
Phil **Pass**	With a skip and a jump but mainly a hop, We're on our way and no-one can stop This grand adventure started by a dare …

Pass   Remind me again why we're going around the pond …
Phil   Because it's there.
Frogs ⎫
Fink   ⎭   They're going around the pond …
Phil (*speaking*) See you in eighty days, Fink.
Frogs ⎫
Fink   ⎭   (*singing*) They must be hopping mad …
Pass (*speaking*) Goodbye, everyone. Wish us luck.

Phil and Pass walk to the side of the stage, pick up the knapsack and cross the stage again, waving goodbye. They exit

Frogs (*singing*)   We wish you luck,
                         But fear the worst,
                         This escapade
                         Would be a first;
                         You've no idea what dangers lie beyond.
                         But in the event that Phil and Pass don't fail,
                         Their story's sure to be a riveting tale,
                         So we hope somehow these fearless frogs prevail
                         Around the pond.

All the Frogs except Fink exit

The Lights dim slightly; the atmosphere is more menacing

Fink looks around, shiftily, then beckons off stage

Fix enters, hissing

Fink Fix. Hey, Fix, get over here, you sneaky snake in the grass. I've got a special job for you that should be right up your street — presuming, of course, you still live on Sleazeball Street.
Fix (*right in Fink's face*) Oh very good, Mr Fink. Sssleazeball Ssstreet. Indeed, yes, sssir.
Fink (*wiping Fix's spittle off his face and trying to get out of range*) There are a couple of foolish frogs trying to journey around the pond. I want you to slow them down a little.
Fix (*getting close to Fink's face again*) Just ssslowed?
Fink (*wiping off more spittle*) Feel free to be creative. If they take a year or two to go around, then fine.
Fix And if they prove ssstubbornly ssswift?
Fink (*managing to dodge the spittle*) Well, let's just say if they never made it back they wouldn't be misssed. Have I made myself clear?

Fix (*into Fink's face again*) Cryssstal.

Fix exits in the direction taken by Phil and Pass. Fink, wiping his face, exits the other way

SCENE 2

The Reed Bed

The Lights brighten, suggesting a sunny day

A chorus of Dragonflies enters

Phil, wearing his knapsack, and Pass enter, walking quite jauntily. They go around in circles during the following song

Song 3: 80 Days (2-6)

Dragonflies (*singing*) Two days out, the reeds they've seen …
Phil ⎫
Pass ⎭ There've been no bad delays …
Dragonflies Further than a frog has been …
Phil ⎫
Pass ⎭ Just like our holidays.

The music slows and so do Phil and Pass. The Lights dim a little

Dragonflies Six days gone, they've come quite far
Phil ⎫
Pass ⎭ This place is like a maze …
Dragonflies But in the reeds they don't know where they are.

The song slows to a stop, as do Phil and Pass. They look up as if the reeds are towering above them

Pass (*speaking*) Phil, let's face it, we're lost. We've been going round in circles for days.
Phil But how can you tell? All these reeds look the same.
Pass (*pointing to someone in the audience – possibly the Head Teacher!*) See that ugly old stump there. We passed it yesterday.
Phil (*looking and shuddering*) Oh, yes, now you mention it — who could forget something as hideously ugly as that?
Pass Makes me feel quite queasy just looking at it.

Phil OK, that settles it, we've no clue where we're going. We need to try and think how to get out of these reeds.

Pass I always think best on a full stomach. (*He looks in the knapsack but is disappointed. He takes out a green party blower and uses it as his tongue to try to catch flies*)

Phil (*taking the knapsack and emptying out some of the contents: a bottle labelled "Frog Tonic", a water mist sprayer marked "Snake Repellent" and some paper napkins*) Trouble is, you've filled your stomach every day and now there's nothing in the bag except a bottle of your mum's frog tonic, some snake repellent and a few napkins.

Pass I'm so weak with hunger I can't catch a single fly. We may as well throw those napkins away.

Phil (*realizing*) Throw them away? That's it. Well done, Pass. (*He starts ripping up napkins*)

Pass What?

Phil We'll use the napkins to leave a trail. That way we can mark where we've been.

Pass Boy, and I didn't even know I was that clever.

Phil puts the bottle of frog tonic in the knapsack. Pass picks up the snake repellent. They exit, leaving a napkin trail

Fix enters and begins picking up the bits of napkin

Fix (*to the audience*) I love my job, and sometimes it's just ssso sssimple.

Fix exits. Phil and Pass enter, dropping bits of napkin. Fix enters, following quite closely behind them, casually collecting napkin pieces

The frogs get to the "ugly stump" again. They point to the audience member and stop

Phil The ugly stump again!

Fix walks into the back of the pair. Phil and Pass turn to see Fix holding the bits of napkin. She tries to hide them behind her back but it's too late

Pass What are you up to, you … you … snake?

Fix Nothing. I'm doing nothing. Honessst.

Pass (*grabbing Fix*) You're lying. You've been following us, picking up the trail we left.

Pass realizes he still has the snake repellent. He sprays it at Fix

Fix Please ssstop! That sssmells disssgusting!

Phil I think you'd better explain yourself. Pass isn't too keen on slitherers — his dad was eaten by one of your kind.

Fix But … But … I'm only being a good sssitizen. Sssomeone's been dropping litter all over the place.

Phil (*shrugging; to Pass*) It makes sense.

Pass She's lying. She speaks with a forked tongue.

Fix But I'm a sssnake — we've all got forked tonguesss.

Pass Oh…Well, I still don't trust her.

Fix Pleassse, Mr Frog. Fix doesn't mean any harm. Fix can be a help. If frogs are leaving a trail it means frogs are lossst. Fix can help them get out of the reedsss.

Phil Really?

Pass Don't trust her, Phileas. You know what her kind are like.

Fix (*pretending to be hurt*) That's what everyone thinksss. Poor me. Poor old Fixxx.

Song 4: Snake in the Grass

Fix (*singing*)	No-one likes a snake in the grass, I just don't know where to begin: Folk find us alarming, Us snakes are seldom charming, 'Cos who would trust a thing that sheds its skin?
Phil **Pass** }	Yuck!
Fix	Who would want a snake as a friend?
Phil **Pass** }	Not us. We find them quite disgusting
Fix	Even I'm ashamed it's who I am.
Phil **Pass** }	But are we right to be mistrusting?
Fix	You don't need a reminder …
Phil **Pass** }	That's right.
Fix	To avoid an old sidewinder …
Phil **Pass** }	They bite.
Fix	And a rattler don't belong in a baby's pram.

Phil and Pass bring out maracas from the knapsack and shake them

Phil ⎫	Who could love a low-down, dirty worm?
Pass ⎬	Slipp'ry cust'mers, shifty and disloyal.
⎭	Those snake eyes they are sure to make you squirm…
Fix	I look in the mirror – even I recoil.
	But tell me …
Fix ⎫	What's wrong with a snake in the grass?
Phil ⎬	They've just had bad press from the start.
Pass ⎭	Why does ev'ryone believe
	That story put about by Eve?
	Then there was Cleo, and the hat-trick
	Was that whole business with St Patrick.
Fix	For me there'll be no kisses,
	Just boos and hisses,
	For this is my given part,
Fix ⎫	But maybe this cold-blooded snake
Phil ⎬	Has got the warmest heart.
Pass ⎭	
Fix	Sssssss…

Fix beckons to Phil and Pass to follow her. They all exit

SCENE 3

A Milk Bar in Wartville

The Lights cross-fade to a setting that suggests a bar interior, with colour and neon effects

A waiter enters, sets up a table and two chairs to one side of the stage and wipes the table with a cloth during the following

The Toadettes enter, dressed biker-chick style, dragging in Phoebe, who is wearing a pretty dress, pretty shoes and pretty ribbons in her hair. The Toadettes look Phoebe up and down, picking at her hair and clothes with disdain as they wonder how to make her look "presentable"

Phoebe You can't treat me like this. I am a royal frog princess. I demand that you toads return me to my people, at once.

Toadette 1 (*ignoring Phoebe*) God, I don't know what the King could see in something like this. She's got no style…

Toadette 2 No class…

Toadette 3 No finesse…

Toadette 4 And she smells funny.

Phoebe How dare you?

Toadette 1 I think it's a frog thing. Anyway, we've got to make something out of her if she's going to be ready for her wedding day.

Phoebe Wedding? My wedding? No, this can't be happening.

The Toadettes surround Phoebe, hiding her from the audience. During the following, the Toadettes dress Phoebe up in a leather jacket and sunglasses

Phil and Pass enter looking a little nervous. They approach the waiter

Phil There you go, Pass. Fix was as good as her word. She got us through the reeds and led us to the toad capital, Wartville.

Pass Yes, but I notice she snuck off when we got to the edge of town. What's wrong with this place?

Phil Don't know. Seems fine to me.

Pass Fine — apart from the terrible stink.

Phil Ssh, it's a toad thing, Pass. I've heard they like a strong aroma. It's almost enough to make you lose your appetite.

Pass Hey, it's not that bad a smell.

Phil *(to Waiter)* Excuse me, waiter, but could we possibly get some food?

Waiter We don't serve frog-kind here in Wartville. Not a single one. Never have. Never will. *(He pauses, then turns to Pass)* So, what can I get you, sir?

Pass Sir? But I'm a ——

Phil clamps his hand over Pass's mouth, realizing that the waiter has mistaken him for a toad

Phil My master, this good *toad* here, would like a large bowl of your finest soup.

Waiter Oh, you're his frog-servant. Why didn't you say so? I'll bring it right over.

The Waiter exits

Phil and Pass go and sit at the table

Phil Just play along, Pass. They obviously think you're a toad, which means we can get some food.

The waiter enters with a large bowl of soup. He puts it down in front of Pass

Pass (*looking at the soup*) Waiter, waiter, there are no flies in my soup.
Waiter (*shaking his head*) It's consommé.

Pass and Phil eat. The Toadettes step aside to reveal Phoebe dressed in leather jacket and sunglasses

Phoebe But it's all some horrible mistake. When my father, the frog king, hears of it he'll be outraged.
Toadette 1 Are you kidding?
Toadette 2 Your father set the whole thing up, lady.
Toadette 3 He lost a lot of money on the Frog Exchange …
Toadette 4 And King Nat made him an offer he couldn't refuse.
Phoebe (*taking off the sunglasses and leather jacket and throwing them at Phil and Pass*) No! My father would never marry me off to some common toad!
Toadette 1 This ain't just some common toad, sister.
Toadette 2 Oh no. This is Nat Natterjack.
Toadette 3 The one…
Toadette 4 The only…
Toadettes King of the Toads.

There is the sound of a motorcycle revving. The Toadettes get very excited

Phoebe Oh no. Please, won't somebody help me?
Phil (*to Pass*) We've got to try and rescue her, Pass.
Pass What? Can't I finish my soup first?
Voice (*booming; off*) Ladies and gentlemen, the King — Nat Natterjack.

Nat enters, dressed like Elvis

The Toadettes swoon

Nat (*in Elvis style*) Uh-huh-huh.

Song 5: King of the Toads

Toadettes (*singing*) Who attracts the biggest flies?
      With a stench like that it's no surprise;
      He's the most
      From coast to coast.
      He's bloated, fat and triple-chinned,
      In these here willows he's the biggest wind;
      He's the best

From east to west.
His odour travels ev'rywhere
'Cos he never washes his underwear.
He's the King, he's the King, he's the King,
The King of the Toads.

Nat Uh-huh-huh …

The Toadettes thrust Phoebe into Nat's arms. She is nearly overcome by the smell

Phil has an idea, which he whispers to Pass. Pass grabs the knapsack, Phil grabs the jacket and sunglasses Phoebe has discarded and they exit

Toadettes   Fungus thrives between his toes
And when he's bored he picks his nose,
It's obscene ——
The size of his green.
His ears are filled up to the top
With more wax than a candle shop,
Navel fluff,
And bad dandruff.
How he got crowned we can't recall,
But we have to love him warts and all,
'Cos he's the King, he's the King, he's the King,
The King of the Toads.

Nat Uh-huh-huh …

Nat dances roughly with Phoebe

Toadettes   His dinner he just loves to slurp,
And always ends with a mighty burp;
Makes us flip
When he lets rip.
He doesn't brush his teeth for weeks,
His breath's so bad it simply reeks,
He's the boss ——
He doesn't floss.
His pores get clogged, his skin explodes,
He don't get snogged 'cos his breath corrodes,
Still he's the King, he's the King, he's the King,
Oh, he's the King, he's the King, he's the King,
Yes, he's the King, he's the King, he's the King,
The King of the Toads…

Nat	Uh-huh-huh…
Toadettes	The King of the Toads …
Nat	Thank you very much …
Toadettes	The King of the Toads …
Nat	That's right.

Pause

Phil enters at a run

Phil Hey, everybody! Have you heard? There's a new kid on the block. The funkiest, fuggiest, fustiest ffff … (*he's going to say "frog", but stops himself*) amphibian in town — Pasper Toad!

Pass enters wearing Phoebe's leather jacket and shades, riding a scooter. He gets off the scooter and sprays himself all over with the snake repellent

The Toadettes smell the air and swoon

Toadette 1 Wow! What's that great new smell?
Pass Ladies, that's *de-toad-erant*.

The Toadettes all sigh and roughly push past Nat to get near Pass. Nat looks downcast

Phil takes the scooter and urges Phoebe to get on the back of it. Phil and Phoebe exit

Toadettes	Toad-ily devoted,
	Toad-ily devoted,
	Toad-ily devoted to him.
Pass/Toadettes	Smell me more,
	Smell me more.
Toadettes	You're the one that we want.

Pass backs slowly towards the exit, waving and blowing kisses. The Toadettes wave after him and swoon helplessly. At the last moment, Pass turns and runs off stage

Voice (*booming; off*) Ladies and gentlemen, Pasper Toad has left the building.

The Toadettes realize their new idol is getting away and give chase. They exit

The waiter and Nat sigh and exit, taking the chairs and table with them

SCENE 4

A rocky shore. Evening

The Lights cross-fade to a dim setting

Phil, Pass and Phoebe stagger on, quite tired

Phoebe I absolutely refuse to swim another stroke. It's unseemly for a princess. Why, I haven't swum since I was a tadpole.

Phil We're far enough away from Wartville. We may as well stop here for the night.

Phoebe Here? On these hard rocks? It's unheard-of for a princess to sleep on stones. I demand that you find me a lily pad — a soft lily pad — a four-poster orchid lily pad — upon which to lay my royal self.

Phil I'm not sure we're going to find anything like that round here, Princess Phoebe.

Phoebe That's just not good enough. You must find a resting place that befits my status. I'll have you know I've got pure green blood.

Pass I'll go look, Phil. The further I get from her whining, the better. No wonder her father sold her off to the first one who would have her.

Pass exits

Phoebe (*to Pass*) My father didn't sell me off! (*To Phil*) And he wasn't the first one who'd have me. I've had lots of suitors. I've had princes and kings begging for my flipper in marriage.

Phil Then why didn't you marry any of them?

Phoebe None of them were good enough for me. But I know that someday I'll find that special someone. Someday my frog prince will come.

Song 6: My One True Frog

(*Singing*)   You've got to kiss a lot of humans
                     To find your one true frog,
                     To fall in love is not as easy
                     As falling off a log.
                     I set my sights so high,
                     But not a single guy
                     Has ever hit the height.
                     I pray that some fine day
                     I'll find my shining knight.

You've got to try a lot of slippers
To find the one that fits,
That Cupid shoots a lot of arrows
But rarely ever hits.
A princess rescue plan
Requires a certain man.
Some girls find heroes, yet,
Just look at what I get.
Most fairy tales are filled with yearning
To reach a happy epilogue,
But, you've got to be bit discerning
To find your one true frog.

Pass (*off; speaking*) Help! Help me!

Pass enters wrapped up in fishing line. He struggles to break free but without success

Phil and Phoebe hurry to help him

Help me out of this fishing line! It's getting tighter and tighter.
Phil Pass, stop struggling. The more you struggle, the tighter the line gets.
Pass But I can't breathe.
Phoebe Help him, Phileas. Bite the wire.

Phil tries to bite through the line but fails

Phil It's no use. This is fishing line. There's nothing that can cut through this.
Pass Please! Somebody!

Song 7: Crayfish

Crayfish (*off; singing*) Crayfish,
                Crayfish,
                Crayfish...

Phil and Phoebe look around to see where the voices are coming from

The Crayfish enter, holding castanets which they snap together like pincers

> Crayfish — don't need strong jaws
> 'Cos crayfish — have got big claws …
> Crayfish — if they hear a yelp
> Then crayfish — we come to your help. Hey!

The music vamps under the following

Lead Crayfish (*speaking*) *Ay caramba!* Cut him free, *amigos.*

The Crayfish gather round Pass and snap their castanets. When they move away, the fishing line is on the floor and Pass is free

> It's a good job we came along, Señor Frog.

Crayfish *Si, si.*

Lead Crayfish Those humans, they are always fishing here and leaving their garbage all over the place.

Crayfish *Si, si.*

Lead Crayfish Only yesterday, me and my cousins, we free a little water vole from a crisp packet. Very sad.

Crayfish *Si, si.*

Pass How can I ever thank you?

Lead Crayfish Don't worry, it's a public service. It's for free.

Crayfish Free, free.

Lead Crayfish *Adios, amigos.* Take care.

Crayfish (*singing*) Crayfish, crayfish,
                Crayfish, crayfish …

The Crayfish exit

The music fades

Phil What lovely crayfish. Who knew crustaceans were so kind? Just goes to show that there are decent types all around the pond.

Pass Unlike whoever set this fishing line to trap me.

Phoebe It wasn't a trap. It was just some careless human. They don't know any better.

Pass I'm not so sure. I couldn't really see in the dark but it felt like the wire was being wrapped around me. And I swear I heard some hissing.

Phoebe Don't be ridiculous.

Phil Hm, travelling at night is a bit dangerous. We should probably rest up till morning.

Phoebe I told you, I couldn't possibly sleep here…

Pass Feel free to go on alone if you want to, Princess.
Phoebe Alone? Oh, maybe I will just close my eyes then.

They sleep

The Lights dim further

The Firefly Chorus enters

Song 8: 80 Days (15)

Firefly Chorus (*singing*) Rest your heads and steal some sleep,
                            But while you rest the hours still creep.
                            Time is marching on and on —
                            For fifteen days and nights have come and gone.

Firefly Chorus exits

The Lights brighten slowly during the rest of the scene to suggest dawn breaking

Fix enters and finds the cut fishing line

Fix Cursesss. Crayfish by the looks of thingsss.

Pass wakes up and sees Fix. He creeps up and grabs her

Pass Got you, you sneaky, slimy snake.

Fix cries out, waking Phil and Phoebe

Fix Let go! You're hurting me!
Phoebe What are you doing to that poor snake, you horrid frog?
Pass I caught her with the fishing line. She must have set the trap for me.
Fix (*thinking quickly*) I was just tidying up the messs. You know what I'm
    like about litter.
Pass A likely story. I know what your kind are like.
Phoebe Let her go, you horrible bully.
Pass She's trying to scupper us, Phil. She's trying to stop us going around
    the pond.
Fix Ssstop you? No. I want to join you. I want to be a part of your exsssiting
    adventure.
Phil (*thinking*) We've got to trust her, Pass. This kind of journey is all about
    making friends. If you don't trust somebody, they are hardly likely to be
    friends with you.

Pass reluctantly lets go of Fix

Fix Thank you, Master Phileasss. If I can be of any asssistance, I would be only too happy.

Phil Well, if you know the lay of the land, you could tell us whether this stony shore continues for very long. The hard going would be very difficult for our flippers.

Fix Oh, these rocks and boulders go on for milesss.

Phil Looks like we're swimming again.

Phoebe No. I simply refuse. I am a noble amphibian. Someone of my standing should not have to swim like some common fish.

Pass Look, lady, if you want to get back home, you'd better start doing the froggy paddle.

Fix Or elssse, you could build a boat.

Phil ⎫
Phoebe ⎬ A boat?

Pass That's ridiculous. It would take ages to build a boat.

Fix But it would sssave time in the long run. Why, a boat could take you all the way around the pond.

Phil thinks about it

Phil Right, that settles it. Let's find some wood and start building.

Phil, Pass, Phoebe and Fix exit in search of wood

SCENE 5

Stickleback Shallows

The Lights cross-fade to a blue wash to give the scene a watery feel

The Sticklebacks (led by Big Stickle but without Little Stickle) enter in a school. They always move in a tightly-packed formation, always on the look-out for possible attackers

Song 9: Stickleback Chorus

Sticklebacks (*singing*) Stickleback, stickleback,
　　　　　　　　Stickle-stickleback,
　　　　　　　　Stickleback, stickleback,
　　　　　　　　Stickle, stickle, stickle,
　　　　　　　　Stickleback, stickleback,
　　　　　　　　Stickle-stickleback,
　　　　　　　　Stickleback...

Little Stickle enters in a panic

Little Stickle He's coming! He's coming! Ol' Pikey's coming after us!

The Sticklebacks panic

Big Stickle Calm down, Sticklebacks. It's impossible. There's no way a fish as big as Ol' Pikey could swim in the shallows.
Little Stickle But it's just like you said, Big Stickle — a great shadow on the water.
Big Stickle Where, Little Stickle?
Little Stickle (*pointing out front*) Out there. Look.

The Sticklebacks gaze out in fear

Big Stickle But that's a boat.
Stickle 1 A boat! A boat! Ol' Pikey's built himself a boat!

The Sticklebacks panic

Big Stickle Don't be silly. Why would a fish build a boat?

The sticklebacks pause and think about this

Little Stickle To get over the shallows.

The Sticklebacks panic

Big Stickle No, no. Look, there are four creatures on that boat.
Stickle 2 Ol' Pikey's brought his friends along to eat us all up!
Big Stickle You're being ridiculous. You can clearly see they are three frogs and a snake.
Stickle 1 Ol' Pikey's disguised himself as a frog!
Little Stickle Or a snake!

There is a big panic amongst the Sticklebacks

Big Stickle Stop this at once, you silly, silly sticklebacks. I will have order in my school. Look, the boat is in trouble. It's run aground on the rocks and seems to be breaking up. We must help them. Everybody follow me.

The Sticklebacks exit and re-enter with Phil, Pass, Phoebe and Fix, all looking a bit bedraggled. They carry bits of a boat, an oar, a lifebelt, etc.

Phil Thank you, Sticklebacks. I don't know what we'd have done without you.

Pass (*pointedly, at Fix*) Drowned, most likely. Thanks to whoever was steering.

Fix Well we would have easily cleared the rocks — if we hadn't been carrying so much extra weight

Pass You watch it, Fix, or I'll fix you good …

Phoebe Now just cut it out, you two. I've had quite enough of your constant bickering.

Big Stickle May I ask where you were heading in that craft of yours?

Phil We are on an epic journey to go around the pond in eighty days.

Little Stickle Ooh, that's quite a way. How long has it taken you to get this far?

Phil This is the thirtieth day.

Big Stickle Thirty days, and you're only this far from Amphibia?

Pass Yes, well, we'd be a lot further if we hadn't been held up building boats and such.

Fix Oh, that's the thanksss I get, is it?

Phoebe As far as I could see, you two arguing about everything took up most of the time.

Phil Hey, you Sticklebacks couldn't tow us a bit further, could you? We could really do with making up some time.

Big Stickle We'd love to help. Really we would. But we daren't leave the safety of the shallows.

Phoebe Why on earth not?

The Sticklebacks look afraid

Little Stickle There's something out there.

Stickle 1 Something dangerous.

Stickle 2 Something deadly.

Sticklebacks Ol' Pikey.

Phil
Pass
Fix   } (*together*)Who?
Phoebe

Big Stickle If you plan to go all the way round this pond, you'd better know what lies ahead.

Song 10: Ol' Pikey

Sticklebacks (*singing*) Stickleback, stickleback,
                              Stickle-stickleback,

Stickleback, stickleback,
Stickle-stickle-stickle,
Stickleback, stickleback,
Stickle-stickleback,
Stickleback.

Let us tell you 'bout Ol' Pikey — King of the Deep,
Ol' Pikey — never asleep,
Ol' Pikey — mean as you like,
Called Pikey — because he's a pike.
And he like to snack on stickleback, stickleback,
Stickle-stickleback,
Stickleback, stickleback,
Stickle-stickle-stickle,
Stickleback, stickleback,
Stickle-stickleback,
Stickleback.

Bred by a boffin who didn't have a clue,
Force-fed radioactive worms, he grew, and he grew.
Ate every fish he considered lesser
Tried to eat the girlfriend of the mad professor,
Scared to go near so they flushed him down the loo.
Ol' Pikey…
Fond of a frog,
Ol' Pikey…
Once ate a dog,
Ol' Pikey…
Big scary fish.
But Ol' Pikey's favourite dish is…
Stickleback, stickleback,
Stickle-stickleback,
Stickleback, stickleback,
Stickle-stickle-stickle,
Stickleback, stickleback,
Stickle-stickleback,
Stickleback.

Down the sewer Pikey made his way
And anything he came across became his prey —
How they'd pray,
He swam into a river with a rumble in his belly.
He ate a shopping trolley and a fisherman's welly,

Big Stickle
Sticklebacks

Little Stickle
Sticklebacks
Stickle 1
Sticklebacks
Stickle 2
Sticklebacks

Big Stickle

Sticklebacks	The angler's looking for his right foot to this day.
	Ol' Pikey…
Little Stickle	Silent and mean,
Sticklebacks	Ol' Pikey…
Stickle 1	A killing machine,
Sticklebacks	Ol' Pikey…
Stickle 2	Better take care,
Sticklebacks	Cos Ol' Pikey's out there somewhere.
	Stickleback, stickleback,
	Stickle-stickleback,
	Stickleback, stickleback,
	Stickle-stickleback,
	Stickleback, stickleback,
	Stickle-stickleback,
	Stickleback, stickleback,
	Stickleback.
	Swam into our pond, began his reign,
	Things will never be the same again —
	Not again.
	In shadowy depths he'll always blend,
Big Stickle	That's why we stay in the shallow end,
Sticklebacks	Though a stickleback hasn't got the biggest brain,
	We know Ol' Pikey's always at the top of our food chain.
	Stickleback.

Phil (*speaking*) Thanks for the warning.

Phoebe We'll make sure we stay clear of the water from now on.

Pass Goodbye, Sticklebacks.

Fix I know a ssshort cut. Everybody follow me.

The Sticklebacks exit one way, Fix the other

Phil Well, gang, better hop to it.

Phil, Pass and Phoebe follow Fix off

SCENE 6

The Swamp

The Lights cross-fade from the blue wash to a bright, sunny setting, possibly with a hint of red, to show it's a hot day

Mosquitoes enter and buzz around; they have kazoos

*Phil, Pass, Phoebe and Fix enter and cross the stage as if wading through a
sticky swamp. They slap themselves as if being bitten by the insects*

Song 11: 80 Days (34-40)

Phil It's so blisteringly hot. And there's just no shade here at all in this
swamp.
Mosquitoes (*singing through the kazoos*) Thirty-four days.
Pass (*speaking*) Some shortcut this turned out to be. The swamp seems to
go on forever.
Phoebe It's so terribly hot and sticky. And my dress is ruined.
Mosquitoes (*singing with kazoos*) Thirty-six days …
Pass (*speaking*) Back in Amphibia now they're probably all sitting in the
shade of the great oak tree …
Phoebe Sipping ice-cold Croaka-cola.
Mosquitoes (*singing with kazoos*) Thirty-eight days …
Fix Maybe we should rest a while — travel later when the sssun's not ssso
hot.
Phil No. Stopping is just what Fink would want us to do. He's probably
measuring up my pad for his furniture as we speak.
Mosquitoes (*singing with kazoos*) Then on the fortieth day …

The Mosquitoes all buzz off as if something is approaching

SCENE 7

Newtopia

*The Lights flash to suggest lightning. There is a clap of thunder. During the
following, the Lights are dim, suggesting overcast skies, and torrential rain
is heard pouring down*

*Phil, Phoebe, Pass and Fix trudge along miserably in the rain. Phil is in the
lead*

Pass Oh well, I guess that's the end of summer.
Phoebe The leaves will be turning soon.
Phil We've got to keep going. Can't let anything get in our way. (*He comes
to a halt as if stopped by something that lies ahead. He looks up in disbelief
as if at a huge mountain off stage*)

Not looking up, the others bump into Phil

Good grief. That is the biggest mountain I've ever seen.

Pass And it seems to be made entirely of broken bottles and tin cans and all kinds of human rubbish.

Phoebe I don't care what you say, there's no way I'm climbing that.

Pass Phoebe, I don't think any of us could possibly climb that.

Fix Oh, what a ssshame. What an awful sssshame. Looks like we're ssstuck. Well, nobody could ever say you didn't give it your best shot, Phileasss.

Phil We're not giving up now, Fix. There must be a way over it.

Pass But Phil, to get over that would take a miracle.

Franklin Newt enters. Like all the newts he carries an umbrella seemingly made from bits of rubbish, carrier bags, magazines, sweet wrappers, food packaging, etc. They wear white lab coats and goggles or large spectacles

Franklin Newt Well, in theory a miracle, but then a miracle is only something which hasn't yet been achieved or created and therefore not in truth a miracle at all — as I believe I proved in my most recent thesis.

Babbage Newt enters from the other side

Babbage Newt And a brilliant thesis it was, Franklin Newt, as I proved in my working model of a miracle, based on your brilliant thesis.

Franklin Newt Why, thank you, Babbage Newt.

Hodgkin Newt and Capability Newt enter

Hodgkin Newt Fellows, do we hear the sound of a think-tank forming?

Capability Newt Or better still, a symposium?

Babbage Newt That would be a logical assumption, Capability Newt.

Franklin Newt But no, we were simply musing on the nature of a miracle ——

The Newts all say "Aaah" very knowingly and stroke their chins

Babbage Newt — and the application of the said miracle through my celebrated working model.

The Newts all nod vigorously

Phil Excuse me, good newts. I'm not sure I understand, but do you mean that you could help us get over that mountain?

Hodgkin Newt Of course we could help you to get over that piffling mountain. We are the most intelligent newts of our generation.

Franklin Newt Precisely, Hodgkin Newt. Every one of us is a scientist or engineer...

Babbage Newt Mathematician…
Capability Newt Or designer…
Hodgkin Newt Goodness, haven't you people ever heard of Newtopia?

Phil and the others are amazed that they've arrived in Newtopia

Pass *This* is Newtopia?
Hodgkin Newt Of course.
Phil The legendary city of the future founded by the famous Isaac Newt?
Franklin Newt The very same.
Phoebe But this place is a dump.

All the Newts are a bit embarrassed

Babbage Newt We haven't quite finished it yet.
Fix You haven't finished? By the looks of things you haven't even ssstarted.
Franklin Newt We are constantly making plans.
Capability Newt Designing things.
Babbage Newt Constructing working models.

There is vigorous chin-stroking and nodding among the Newts

Hodgkin Newt It's just that we can never quite agree on the fine details, so
we never actually get anything built.
Phil Oh well. (*Trying to bluff the Newts into helping*) If you, the most brilliant
newts of your generation, can't help us then we'd better think of another
way of conquering the mountain. (*To the gang*) Maybe we should try
asking the fish?

Phil and the gang start to leave

Babbage Newt Fish? Fish?!
Hodgkin Newt Wait. Don't go. Building the perfect city takes years of
tireless planning and unceasing deliberation. Making a simple machine to
fly three frogs and a snake over a mountain, why, it would only take a day
at the most.
Babbage Newt An afternoon.
Franklin Newt A couple of hours.
Capability Newt We could do it in our sleep.

Song 12: Rise Up Toward the Sun

Newts (*singing*) We can solve this simple problem
                              Building a machine that flies,

Hodgkin Newt   It will need a big propeller,
Babbage Newt   Wings to take it to the skies,
Franklin Newt   It should be aerodynamic
Capability Newt And have fins to keep it true,
Hodgkin Newt   We could steer it with a joystick,
Babbage Newt   Then when we have finished, paint it blue …
Hodgkin Newt   No, paint it red …
Franklin Newt   No, paint it yellow …
Capability Newt Pink …
Hodgkin Newt   Green …
Babbage Newt   Gold …
Franklin Newt   Lilac …
Capability Newt Orange …
Hodgkin Newt   Ochre …
Babbage Newt   Purple …
Phil (*speaking*) Stop! Look, I don't know much about building a flying
machine but I'll tell you what I do know …
              (*Singing*) You've got to have co-operation, before you get things
                          done,
                          And then you need communication, a voice for everyone,
                          And if you have harmonization, and you walk before you
                          run
                          You'll find that this little nation will rise up toward the
                          sun.
Hodgkin Newt (*speaking*) Thank you, Mr Frog. We were losing sight of the
big picture. Come, Newts, let us put aside our differences and concentrate
on getting this thing off the ground.
Newts (*singing*) We can solve this simple problem,
                       Send you soaring in the air,
                       But with added safety features
                       To make sure you fly with care,
Babbage Newt   Every seat will have a belt …
Franklin Newt   With breathing masks above your head,
Capability Newt Exits rear and centre …
Hodgkin Newt   Coloured lights along the floor all flashing red …
Babbage Newt   No, flashing blue …
Franklin Newt   No, flashing yellow …
Capability Newt Pink …
Hodgkin Newt   Green …
Babbage Newt   Gold …
Franklin Newt   Lilac …
Capability Newt Orange …
Hodgkin Newt   Ochre…

Babbage Newt   Purple...
Phil   ⎫   Stop!
Pass   ⎪   You've got to have co-operation, before you get things
Fix   ⎬   done,
Phoebe   ⎭   And then you need communication, a voice for everyone,
                     And if you have harmonization, and you walk before you
                        run,
                     You'll find that this little nation will rise up toward the
                        sun.

The Lights brighten; the sun is coming out

Hodgkin Newt (*speaking*) Hey, newts! It's finally stopped raining.
Babbage Newt And the sun is coming out.
Franklin Newt That will lead to a refraction of the light through the water
     droplets and create a ... yes, look!
Capability Newt It's a rainbow!
Newts (*singing*)   We can solve these simple problems,
                     Nature's given us a clue,
                     We are blessed with many colours,
                     We should value ev'ry hue,
                     Be it red, yellow, pink, green,
                     Gold, lilac, orange or blue.
Phil   ⎫   'Cos when you've got ——
Pass   ⎪   Co-operation, you're bound to get things done,
Fix   ⎬   Especially with communication, a voice for everyone,
Phoebe   ⎪   And if you have harmonization, and you walk before you
Newts   ⎭   run,
                     You'll find that this little nation will rise up toward the sun

The Newts drag on various bits of junk, including a balloon basket
(possibly made up to look like a margarine tub), helium balloons with
sweet wrappers and crisp packets stuck on them, and umbrellas, and make
a flying machine. Phil, Pass, Fix and Phoebe climb aboard and twirl the
umbrellas like propellers

Hodgkin Newt   All together now ——
Phil   ⎫
Pass   ⎪
Fix   ⎬   — co-operation ——
Phoebe   ⎪
Newts   ⎭

Babbage Newt   — and then you need ——
Phil ⎫
Pass ⎪
Fix   ⎬   — communication ——
Phoebe ⎪
Newts ⎭
Franklin Newt   — with a bit of ——
Phil ⎫
Pass ⎪
Fix   ⎬   — harmonization ——
Phoebe ⎪
Newts ⎭
Capability Newt — QED.
Phil ⎫
Pass ⎪
Fix   ⎬   This little nation will rise up toward the sun.
Phoebe ⎪
Newts ⎭
Franklin Newt (*speaking*) The balloon will give you enough lift to take you over the mountain and far beyond.

Phil Thank you very much for your help.

Hodgkin Newt No, thank you, Phileas. Now we're all pulling together, we're sure to get Newtopia built.

The Newts look up as if the machine is taking off

Capability Newt Good luck.

Babbage Newt They're going to need it. We never did get my working model to work.

Pass What did he say?

Phil ⎫   (*singing*) You've got to have co-operation, before you get
Pass ⎪   things done,
Fix   ⎬   And then you need communication, a voice for everyone,
Phoebe ⎪   And if you have harmonization, and you walk before you
Newts ⎭   run,
                   You'll find that this little nation will rise up toward the
                        sun.
                   This little nation sure will have a lot of fun,
                   This little nation will rise up toward the sun.

The Newts exit backwards, waving upwards toward the rising balloon

The Lights dim on the Newts but remain bright on Phil and the gang in the balloon

The Balloon Flight

There is the sound of the wind blowing

Phil, Phoebe, Pass and Fix sway gently in the basket

Pass Wow, everything seems so small from up here. Those creatures down there look just like ants.

Fix Those creatures *are* ants, you sssimpleton.

Pass (*defensively*) Well, those ants look just like — really tiny ants.

Phoebe Oh, Phileas, this is turning out to be such an amazing adventure. When I was living in the palace, being waited upon hand and flipper, being protected and cosseted and spoilt rotten, I never dreamed I would one day get to have a thrilling adventure, travel to distant places and meet fabulous new people.

Phil And I never dreamed I would get to ride over a glass and tin mountain in a flying machine built by newts with my best friend and a snake and a beautiful princess.

Phoebe (*checking her hair — it's a mess*) Beautiful?

Phil and Phoebe smile awkwardly at each other

Pass Hey, Phil, we're safely over the mountain.

Phil What's that on the other side? It looks like a waterfall.

Phoebe Don't mention falling when we're this high up.

Phil Don't worry, Phoebe, this balloon is perfectly safe

Off stage, the chorus hiss like a balloon deflating

Pass (*curiously*) Then what's that hissing noise?

Phil, Pass and Phoebe look at Fix

Fix Why are you looking at me? It's nothing to do with me.

Phil Well, if the hissing isn't you it must mean …Oh no! (*He looks up*) We've sprung a leak!

They sway wildly in the basket. Pass grabs Fix

Phoebe We're falling!

Pass You did it, didn't you? I knew we should never trust you.

Fix I'm innosssent, I tell you. I was only wondering what that little valve did.
Phoebe We're going to crash!
Phil Hold on everybody!

They all scream. Black-out

During the following, the Wavemakers enter with long strips of blue fabric. They stretch the strips of fabric across the front of the stage and ripple them to simulate the surface of the pond. At the back of the stage, one wavemaker holds a pole from which hangs a strip curtain, to simulate a waterfall

The basket of the balloon is set up in the centre of the pond, upturned, as if it has crashed there, the four travellers with it, Phil and Pass on the basket, Fix and Phoebe in the water

A spotlight comes up on a Fisherman sitting to one side of the stage. He is "fishing" into the audience. He spots something high up in the air and traces its descent as it falls into the pond

There comes the faint sound of Phil, Pass, Phoebe and Fix screaming as they fall — followed by a large splash

Fisherman (*to the audience*) Now, that's something you don't see every day.

The spotlight on the Fisherman fades and blue lighting comes up on the rest of the stage

SCENE 9

The Waterfall

Phil and Pass sit on the upturned basket while Fix struggles in the waves. Phoebe is as yet not visible

Fix Help! Sssave me!
Phil (*holding out his hand*) Grab hold, Fix.
Pass Don't help her, Phil. It's her fault we crashed.
Phil We can't just let her drown, Pass. Give me a hand.

Pass reluctantly helps Phil drag Fix on to the basket

Fix Thank you. Oh, thank you, Master Phileasss. But where's Phoebe?
Phil I don't know. Can anyone see her?
Pass There she is!

Phoebe comes up for air between the waves. She is struggling to keep her head above water

Phil Phoebe! Over here!

Phil, Pass and Fix look around anxiously. Then, from between the strips of the curtain comes a large fin which moves between the waves

Pass Oh no. Remember what the sticklebacks said about the waterfall?
Phil ⎫
Pass ⎬ (*together*) Ol' Pikey!
Fix ⎭

They urge Phoebe to swim to them quickly. The fin moves closer to Phoebe

Phoebe Help! Help!

Song 13: The Waterfall

Wavemakers (*singing*)   Ol' Pikey ...
Phil (*speaking*) I'll save you, Phoebe!
Wavemakers (*singing*)   Ol' Pikey ...

Phil jumps into the waves and helps Phoebe towards the basket. Pass and Fix help her climb on top

The fin heads towards Phil who is still in the water

Pass (*speaking*) Phil! Watch out! He's right behind you!
Wavemakers (*singing*)   Ol' Pikey ...
Fix (*speaking*) I can't bear to look!
Wavemakers (*singing*)   Ol' Pikey...
                                Pikey, Pikey, Pikey, Pikey
                                Pikey, Pikey, Pikey, Pikey,
                                Pikey, Pikey, Pikey, Pikey...

The fin approaches Phil at speed. Phil turns, sees the fin and raises his arms to try and protect himself

Black-out

A spotlight comes up on the Fisherman at the side of the stage. He is struggling with something big on the end of his line. He reels in his line and on the end is a large fish — Ol' Pikey

Fisherman At last I've got you, you big ugly pike!

The spotlight fades to Black-out

The Fisherman and the Wavemakers exit

Phil lies C, unconscious, his knapsack beside him, and Pass, Phoebe and Fix gather round him

Scene 10

On the Bank

The Lights come back up, but are quite subdued

Pass Is he going to be all right?

Phoebe I don't know, Pass.

Pass Why won't he wake up?

Phoebe He's just been bitten and battered and dragged under by the biggest, baddest fish in the pond. It's a wonder he's alive at all.

Pass (*to Fix*) This is all your fault. You've been trying to stop us every step of the way. You got us lost in the reeds. You tangled me up in that fishing line. You wrecked our boat in the shallows. You sabotaged the balloon and now Phil has ended up badly hurt.

Phoebe Fix, is this true?

Fix No, no, no, no, no! Well, yes. Look, Fink employed me to help him win the bet so I was just trying to ssslow you down.

Pass I could wring your neck. (*He grabs Fix by the neck*)

Fix (*being choked*) I never really meant any harm. I'm ssso sssorry. I'd do anything to fix things.

Phoebe (*stopping Pass*) Pass, fighting is not going to get us anywhere. Phileas is the important thing. We've got to pull together or else he's going to … Well, let's not even think about that. Pass, why don't you go off and find some food? Phileas will need nourishment when he wakes up. Fix and I will watch over him.

Pass Yes, well, just make sure you keep a watch over her as well.

Pass exits reluctantly

Fix I feel terrible for what I did. You all treated me ssso well and this is how I repay you. Do you think Pass and Phil will ever forgive me?

Phoebe Of course, Fix. That's what friends do.

No-one's called Fix a friend before

Fix Friends?

Phoebe Yes, friends. Friends don't judge you because of the mistakes you make, or how you look, or anything like that. Friends see what's inside. And inside that sneaky skin, I just know there's a good honest snake bursting to get out.

Fix Thank you, Phoebe. Look, I'm going to go and try to patch things up with Pass. Are you going to be OK here?

Phoebe Sure. I'm certain all Phileas needs is a rest. He's getting a bit of colour back in his cheeks now.

Fix (*trying to be positive*) Yes, you're right. He's looking a lot greener.

Fix exits

Phoebe (*stroking Phil's forehead*) Please wake up, Phileas.

Phoebe looks in Phil's knapsack which is lying next to him and finds the bottle of frog tonic. She pours some into his mouth but still he doesn't wake. In desperation, she decides she must try something. She looks both ways to check no-one is watching, puckers up her lips then leans down to kiss him. At that moment, Phil wakes up

Phil (*thinking he's still fighting Ol' Pikey*) Get off me, you big ugly fish! (*He realizes it's Phoebe*) Oh, God, Phoebe. Gosh, I'm really sorry.

Phoebe (*pretending to be offended*) Well, that's a fine thing to call a princess. (*Softening*) But as you saved my life I suppose I'll have to forgive you.

Phil What am I doing?! I shouldn't be lying around here. (*He tries to stand but is still groggy from the fight with Ol' Pikey and falls back down*)

Phoebe You're in no shape to go anywhere. Don't worry. You've got plenty of time. There's still twenty days before you're due back in Amphibia. And you can't go anywhere until you've got your strength back.

Phil lies back. He seems quite happy not to be going anywhere just yet

Fix enters, all of a fluster

Fix Phoebe. Phileas. You must come quickly. It's Pass. He's been arrested by the water ratsss.

Phil
Phoebe } (*together*) What?!

Phil stands shakily. Phoebe steadies him and they all exit

SCENE 11

A Courtroom in Ratsburg

The Lights cross-fade to a harsh white setting to suggest the interior of a courtroom

The Prosecutor and Water Rats enter, dragging in Pass

During the following song the Water Rats set up a table and chair as the judge's bench

Song 14: 80 Days (60 – 70)

Prosecutor ⎫
Water Rats ⎬ (*singing*) Sixty days, he's thrown in jail …
Pass (*speaking*) What did I do? What did I do?
Prosecutor ⎫
Water Rats ⎬ (*singing*) Sixty-one, no chance of bail …
Pass (*speaking*) I want to see my lawyer!

Lawyer Rat enters

Prosecutor ⎫
Water Rats ⎬ (*singing*) Sixty-two and here's his brief…
Lawyer Rat (*speaking*) Goodness, I'm looking forward to this. It's my first case.
Prosecutor ⎫
Water Rats ⎬ (*singing*) Sixty-three, he's charged with being a thief.

Phil, Phoebe and Fix enter and speak to Pass

Phil (*speaking*) Apparently you've been charged with catching flies without a licence.
Pass When did a frog ever need a licence to catch a fly?
Phoebe We're in Ratsburg now, Pass. They seem to have a law about everything.
Phil And I'm afraid they're pretty harsh on people who break them.
Prosecutor ⎫
Water Rats ⎬ (*singing*) Sixty-seven, sixty-eight …
Lawyer Rat (*speaking*) I think our best chance is to plead insanity.
Prosecutor ⎫
Water Rats ⎬ (*singing*) Sixty-nine, they've set the date.

Pass (*speaking*) I want to change my lawyer.

Prosecutor ⎱
Water Rats ⎰ (*singing*) Seventy days and what's his fate?

Fix (*speaking*) We'll defend you, Pass.

Prosecutor ⎱
Water Rats ⎰ (*singing*) Soon we'll know for here's the magistrate.

Judge Rat enters with his gavel, which he bangs on the table

Judge Rat Order! Order! I will have no singing in my court! Prosecutor, are you ready with your charges?

Prosecutor Yes, m'lud. It is our intention to prove that on Wednesday last, the defendant did openly, and with flagrant disregard for the law, gather and consume more than 100 assorted insects of the flying variety.

Water Rats (*shocked*) Ooh.

Prosecutor Out of season!

Water Rats (*more shocked*) Ooh.

Prosecutor Without a licence!

There is uproar among the Water Rats

Water Rat 1 Send him down!

Water Rat 2 Lock him up!

Water Rat 3 Throw away the key!

Judge Rat (*banging gavel*) Order! Order!

Pass looks very worried. Phil, Phoebe and Fix huddle together to try and think of a defence

Prosecutor The prosecution calls as its one and only witness, the defendant. (*To Pass*) Do you promise to tell the truth, the whole truth and nothing but the truth, so help you, frog?

Pass (*with a gulp*) I suppose so.

Prosecutor Did you, on Wednesday last, engage in the illegal act of gathering and consuming over one hundred assorted insects of the flying variety — out of season — without a licence?

Pass I suppose so. But ——

Prosecutor There you have it. Condemned from his own mouth. The prosecution rests.

There is uproar among the Water Rats

Water Rat 1 Make an example of him!

Water Rat 2 Flogging's too good!

Water Rat 3 Bring back hanging!

Judge Rat (*banging gavel*) Order! Order! Well, it all seems clear cut to me. This is a most terrible crime and I feel I must bring the harshest sentence to bear.

Fix (*pushing Phil forward*) Wait, Your Honour. My friend has something to add to the cassse.

Phil (*to Fix*) I do?

Judge Rat Well?

Phil Er, well, shouldn't the defendant be allowed — a defence?

Judge Rat Oh. Yes, I suppose we might as well make it all above board. Although for the life of me I can't think what on earth you could say to convince us of his innocence.

Song 15: The Pursuit of Flies

Phil	(*singing*) You see a squirrel stealing nuts in autumn,
	You wouldn't ever think to lock him up,
	A fox snacks on a hen, there's no enquiry or post-mortem
	And a cow can chew on any buttercup …
Phoebe **Fix**	(*together*) Buttercup, buttercup.
Phil	'Cos animals obey the laws of nature,
	Maggots have a feast when something dies,
	A rat could eat a frog, I wouldn't hate ya,
	'Cos I believe in life, liberty, and …
Water Rats	And what?
Phil	The pursuit of flies.
All	The pursuit of flies, the pursuit of … ooh.
Phoebe	You wouldn't show a warrant in a warren
	If a rabbit had purloined a lettuce leaf.
	A migratory bird isn't held for being foreign
	And a magpie can't be charged with being a thief.
Phil **Fix**	Not a thief, not a thief.
Phoebe **Phil** **Fix**	These truths are held for every single creature, A binding contract which to all applies, Read Mother Earth's own statutes they will teach ya,
Phil **Fix**	Teach ya …
Phoebe	All 'bout life …
Water Rats **Phil** **Fix**	Life …

Phoebe	Liberty …
Water Rats ⎫	
Phil ⎬	Liberty …
Fix ⎭	
Phoebe	And …
Water Rats ⎫	
Phil ⎬	And what?
Fix ⎭	
Phoebe	The pursuit of flies.
All	The pursuit of flies,
	The pursuit of flies,
	The pursuit of flies.

Judge (*speaking*) Order! I'm sorry, but the laws of Ratsburg are clear on this matter.

Fix But Your Honour, this isn't just about Ratsburg, it's about the universal law which governs us all …

(*Singing*) For come that judgement day
You'll meet that great rat in the sky,
Answer true and claim your own eternal prize.
So when he asks you what your creed is
Look him squarely in the eye,
And testify …

Water Rats ⎫	
Prosecutor ⎭	Testify …
Phil ⎫	
Phoebe ⎬	You believe in life…
Fix ⎭	
Judge	Life …
Phil ⎫	
Phoebe ⎬	Liberty …
Fix ⎭	
Judge	Liberty …
Phil ⎫	
Phoebe ⎬	And …
Fix ⎭	
Judge	And what?
Phil ⎫	
Phoebe ⎬	You believe in life…
Fix ⎭	
Water Rats ⎫	
Judge ⎬	Life…
Prosecutor ⎭	

Phil **Phoebe** **Fix**	Liberty...
Water Rats **Judge** **Prosecutor**	Liberty...
Phil **Phoebe** **Fix**	And ...
Water Rats **Judge** **Prosecutor**	Tell us more.
Phil **Phoebe** **Fix**	You believe in life ...
Water Rats **Judge** **Prosecutor**	Life ...
Phil **Phoebe** **Fix**	Liberty ...
Water Rats **Judge** **Prosecutor**	Liberty ...
Phil **Phoebe** **Fix**	And...
Water Rats **Judge** **Prosecutor**	And what?
Phil **Phoebe** **Fix**	The pursuit of flies.
All	The pursuit of flies, The pursuit of flies, The pursuit of flies, The pursuit of flies, The pursuit of ——

Judge (*speaking*) Not guilty!
All   (*singing*) — of flies!

The Last Leg of the Journey

The Lights soften to sunnier tones

The Water Rats exit with the table and chairs; the gang waves goodbye to them

Pass I don't know how to thank you. (*To Fix*) All of you. If you hadn't defended me …

Phil There's no time for that now, Pass. The leaves are starting to fall.

Phoebe And there's only ten days left.

Fix Then what are we waiting for?

Pass
Fix } (*together*) Let's hop to it!
Phoebe

Song 16: 80 Days (71 – 79)

During the song, Phil, Phoebe, Pass and Fix run on the spot, as if running around the pond

Various creatures featured throughout the show enter and go past, waving to them

Phil
Phoebe
Pass } (*singing*) We're jogging round the pond.
Fix

Creatures Seventy-one days, seventy-two,
Eight days left now, way too few,

Phil
Phoebe
Pass } We're running round the pond …
Fix

Creatures Seventy-three days, seventy-four,
Leaves are falling to the floor…

Fix stumbles and Pass helps her

Phil
Phoebe
Pass } We're racing 'round the pond…
Fix

Creatures Seventy-five, six, seven and eight
Maybe they won't be too late …

Phil	⎫
Phoebe	We're sprinting round the pond…
Pass	
Fix	⎭
Creatures	But then on the seventy-ninth day
	All hope's gone 'cause something's in their way.

Phil, Phoebe, Pass and Fix come to an abrupt halt having seen something in front of them. They pant, out of breath

The Creatures exit

There is the sound of fast-running water

Pass Oh, no. The weir is in full flow because of the autumn rains. We'll never swim that.

Phoebe This can't be happening. Not when we're so close.

Fix I can see Amphibia over the other ssside. There has to be a way.

The others turn to Phil

Phil No. There's no other way. (*He sits down, dejected*) That's it. I've failed. Fink was right — it is impossible to go around the pond in eighty days. There goes the bet. There goes everybody's week off. There goes my luxury pad.

Black-out

Phil, Phoebe, Pass and Fix exit and the Frogs and Fink enter

A lone leaf is set, suspended above the stage

SCENE 13

Amphibia

The Lights come up; the sunny colours of the last scene have given way to autumnal reds

The Frogs are waiting expectantly, looking off stage for a sign of Phil. Fink checks his fob watch and looks up at the lone leaf

Fink Well, frogs, you can cancel any holiday plans for this week. The eighty days are almost up and there's no sign of our intrepid adventurers. But as a special treat, you can all stay after work and help me move my furniture into Phileas's luxury pad.

Frog 1 You know, I really thought they were going to make it.

Frog 2 I guess the pond is just too big.

Fink I tried to warn young Phileas of the dangers, but he's always been a headstrong frog.

Frog 3 I wonder if we'll ever see Phil and Pass again.

Fink Something tells me they've come to a sssticky end.

Frog 4 But Mr Fink, there's still one leaf left on the Great Oak.

Fink Really? (*He looks up*)

The leaf falls, making a slow, drifting descent towards the ground

(*Laughing*) Oh yes, but look — it's starting to fall.

Song 17: Around the Pond (*Reprise*)

Frogs	They started round the pond,
	Some eighty days ago,
	And did they make it round?
Fink	I'm afraid the answer's n...
Sticklebacks (off)	Stickleback, stickleback,
	Stickle-stickleback,
	Stickleback, stickleback,
	Stickle, stickle, stickle...

The sticklebacks enter pulling a raft upon which ride Phil, Pass, Phoebe and Fix

The leaf falls right into the outstretched arms of Pass. The Frogs cheer

Phil Made it just in time. Thanks, Sticklebacks.

Big Stickle No, thank you, Phileas. With Ol' Pikey gone, we can swim wherever we want.

Pass (*handing leaf to Fink*) Keep this as a souvenir, Fink, because you're not getting your hands on anyone's pad.

Fink (*to Fix*) Snake, I thought you were supposed to *fix* things.

Fix Sorry, Mr Fink, but that's what you get for trusting a sssnake in the grasss. (*She spits in Fink's face*)

Phil I believe, Mr Fink, you owe everyone a week off.

The Frogs cheer

Fink But it's a busy time of year ... I can't do all that riveting on my own ... It's not possible.

Phil Well, Fink, in my experience, you just don't know what's possible until you try.

Phoebe Now, I suggest we throw a big party in that luxury pad I've heard so much about.

Phil Good idea, Phoebe. And everyone's invited.

They all cheer — apart from Fink

Fink (*speaking*) God, I hate a "hoppy" ending.

Frogs **Sticklebacks**	They went around the pond,
Phil **Pass** **Phoebe** **Fix**	Around the pond, around the pond,
Frogs **Sticklebacks**	As if without a care,
Phil **Pass** **Phoebe** **Fix**	Not a care, not a care,
All	With a skip and a jump but mainly a hop, They went their way and no-one could stop This journey far into the great beyond. They'll tell us tales of things that they have seen, From here to there and everywhere in between, It took them eighty days but they have been — Around the pond.

CURTAIN

FURNITURE AND PROPERTY LIST

<small>SCENE 1</small>

On stage: Lunchboxes for **Frogs**
Extra large lunchbox for **Pass** containing baguette
Knapsack containing green party blower, bottle labelled "Frog Tonic", water mist sprayer marked "Snake Repellent", paper napkins, maracas

Personal: **Fink**: fob watch

<small>SCENE 2</small>

See Staging Suggestions p. iv

<small>SCENE 3</small>

Off stage: Table and chairs (**Waiter**)
Large bowl of soup (**Waiter**)
Scooter (**Pass**)

Personal: **Waiter**: cloth

<small>SCENE 4</small>

See Staging Suggestions p. iv

Personal: Fishing line (**Pass**)
Castanets (**Crayfish**)

<small>SCENE 5</small>

See Staging Suggestions p. iv

Off stage: Bits of a boat, oars, lifebelt etc. (**Sticklebacks**)

<small>SCENE 6</small>

No additional props

SCENE 7

See Staging Suggestions p. iv

Off stage: Umbrellas seemingly made of rubbish (**Newts**)
                 Balloon basket, helium balloons with sweet wrappers and crisp
                 packets stuck on them, umbrellas (**Newts**)

SCENE 8

See Staging Suggestions p. iv

During lighting change p. 31

Set: Long strips of blue fabric, pole with strip curtain for **Wavemakers**
                 Fishing rod for **Fisherman**

Re-set: Balloon basket upturned as if it has crashed

SCENE 9

Off stage: Large fin (**Stage Management**)

SCENE 10

No additional props

SCENE 11

Off stage: Table and chair (**Water Rats**)

Personal: **Judge Rat**: gavel

During lighting change p.41

Set: Lone leaf suspended above stage

SCENE 12

No additional props

SCENE 13

See Staging Suggestions p. iv

LIGHTING PLOT

To open: Darkness

Cue 1	The sixth "Rivet" *Gradually bring up general exterior lighting*	(Page 1)
Cue 2	All the **Frogs** except **Fink** exit *Dim lights to menacing setting*	(Page 6)
Cue 3	**Fix** and **Fink** exit *Brighten lights to sunny day exterior setting*	(Page 7)
Cue 4	Music slows; **Phil** and **Pass** slow *Dim lights slightly*	(Page 7)
Cue 5	**Fix**, **Phil** and **Pass** exit *Cross-fade to bar interior setting*	(Page 10)
Cue 6	**Waiter** and **Nat** exit with chairs and table *Cross-fade to dim setting*	(Page 15)
Cue 7	**Phil**, **Pass** and **Phoebe** sleep *Dim lights further*	(Page 18)
Cue 8	**Firefly Chorus** exits *Gradually brighten lights to suggest dawn breaking*	(Page 18)
Cue 9	**Phil**, **Pass**, **Phoebe** and **Fix** exit *Cross-fade to blue wash*	(Page 19)
Cue 10	**Phil**, **Pass** and **Phoebe** follow **Fix** off *Cross-fade to a bright, sunny exterior setting,* *possibly with a hint of red*	(Page 23)
Cue 11	**Mosquitoes** all buzz off *Flash to suggest lightning, then dim,* *"overcast" exterior lighting*	(Page 24)
Cue 12	**Phil**, **Pass**, **Fix** and **Phoebe**: " ... toward the sun." *Brighten to sunny exterior setting*	(Page 28)

EFFECTS PLOT

www.ingramcontent.com/pod-product-compliance
Lightning Source LLC
LaVergne TN
LVHW051806080426
835511LV00019B/3423